LESSN

SS
SNESS

AHSAHTA PRESS
THE NEW SERIES #40

LESSNESS

BRIAN HENRY

AHSAHTA PRESS
BOISE, IDAHO 2011

Ahsahta Press, Boise State University
Boise, Idaho 83725-1525
http://ahsahtapress.boisestate.edu
http://ahsahtapress.boisestate.edu/books/henry2/henry2.htm

Printed in the United States of America
Cover design by Quemadura
Book design by Janet Holmes
First printing March 2011

Library of Congress Cataloging-in-Publication Data

Henry, Brian, 1972-
Lessness / Brian Henry.
p. cm. -- (The new series ; #40)
ISBN-13: 978-1-934103-20-3 (pbk. : alk. paper)
ISBN-10: 1-934103-20-9 (pbk. : alk. paper)
I. Title.
PS3608.E566L47 2011
811'.6--DC22   201004382

ACKNOWLEDGMENTS AND NOTES

Written between 1995 and 2008, these poems owe much to Tara Rebele, Andrew Zawacki, Tomaž Šalamun, and John Kinsella.

Thank you to the editors of the following publications, in which some of these poems first appeared, occasionally in different form and/or under different titles: *American Poetry Review, Boston Review, Colorado Review, Columbia, Denver Quarterly, Elixir, English Language Notes, Fascicle, Free Verse, Fulcrum, Jacket* (Australia), *Luna, Lyric Poetry Review, Metre* (Ireland), *New American Writing, Notre Dame Review, Oxford Poetry* (UK), PEN's *Public Lives/Private Lives, Poetry Northwest, Poetry Review* (UK), *Southwest Review, Washington Square, Western Humanities Review,* and *The Wolf* (UK). Special thanks to *Beloit Poetry Journal* for publishing the original 13-part "Wreckage" in its entirety, and to *Poetry Daily* for reprinting part of the sequence. "Tornado / Warning" also appeared on *Verse Daily.* "Broken tooth" was reprinted in *Notre Dame Review: The First Ten Years* (University of Notre Dame Press, 2009) and in *The Fifth Question and After: Poems for Tomaž Šalamun,* edited by Kevin Hart (Sydney: Vagabond, 2001). "Map / Less" also appeared (as "Map") in *Voices for Kosovo,* edited by Rupert Loydell (Devon: Stride, 1999).

The proem begins with the end of John Kinsella's *Graphology* (Equipage, 1997). "Map / Less" is for Tomaž Šalamun. The title of "Err Far" is from St. Augustine's *Confessions.* "Thank You for the Epiphany" was written during Ronald Reagan's funeral-orgy. "Beside Myself Refusing Myself" is for Ethan Paquin. "Elegy, Post-Paternal" is in memory of Donald R. Burgess. "Wreckage" leans on Philippe Lacoue-Labarthe's *Poetry as Experience* as well as John Berger's *Ways of Seeing. Lessness* is conceived as a companion volume to *Graft* (New Issues, 2003).

Contents

for John Kinsella

To strike out across the dusty paddocks where the possibility of moisture

declares itself

a quaquaversal diviner, the hindered align themselves with those who carry

squandered posture

from one extreme to the other in this corral of miracles & mishaps.

"Lapidary"

does not contain the land or its scape, & lessons in traction that omit grip, tread,

or charts of slopes

reduce the science to guesswork, hunch & skull-scratch, a lapsus in praxis that stakes

action on bed-

lam when the asylum of system can gauge the hill & guarantee quick passage.

Land always breaks

along well-defined measures, & fountains will rise through miles of stone & salt to offer

advice, presage

some fall or another, or play oracle to every settler who needs water,

not weather fore-

casts or fortunes told: this locus of wreckage is secular, slick with crystals &

prone to barter—

when everything is free, the market untouched by such coaxing, mountains can be bought

for flame-blown sand

that arraigns its holders in self-portraits framed by tussock, wheat & hills that go white

in the onslaught

of wind that haggles so fierce it levels the trading fields to salt & salt's gestures.

I.

My nation is a pasture horseless in demeanor,
its contours ignite happenstance from harm-
lessness less distant in manner.
Thrush appointed to hold truck with the pasture
nourish the pasture.
Shares hired to counsel the pasture
thresh the pasture.
When the shape of the sound stripping the wind
builds a wall at the edge of the pasture,
it rehearses last rites
for this burden drained by distance:

Walllessness should not be considered a harm
or lack, but a willingness to counsel
& receive counsel from horses
in a horseless nation,
where the pasture remains as reminder, reminding
the horses of what's remained
& what remains for the horses.

Just Rain

& something like a tree shuddered into view

a made thing on crutches snow collapsing all around it

the tree will remain nameless the snow will melt the grass

nourished by the snow if you remove the tree pull it

by its roots the branching roots that disturb the soil's hold

the hole's purpose unknown its depth & span

seeded or not the hole will spawn something

like grass a mushroom cluster on the shadow side

climbing in you will find what nearly pierced you blind

a writhing clump of termites so white they glow

you could crush them the sacks they carry

or flood them (with poison) (with rain) the result

will be the same the sudden deaths will flare

ruin your eyes for good your head will shrink

melt or decompose

Subterra

*

Beyond the scarred birds

                            against the soft dome

engines   the light into filaments &

        the fissures of

                            but flesh

                *

        The few who remained on the surface
        hear the churning below,
        call it *terremoto*   *demons* or *ghosts*
        of those lost before
        the oldest among them was born: the sound
        less sound than pressure
        swelling the ground into waves   furniture
        & knickknacks, floors, bikes
        & cars tremble at the touch of   a girl
        has vanished   swallowed.

*

the cable shimmied through the socket

                        a white no bones
could own up to

                *

                                grabs
nothing that does not pray for capture

                        one eye blinks while the other holds

                                trembles
at the smell of failure
                        on a man's fingers

Up There

On a hill where
air grows
the perfect man.

Scar

~~To see a body thrown beyond its boundaries~~

~~To fly & learn the bones have no borders~~

~~Flesh a wedge to hold the air in place~~

~~The air dilating to keep the span intact~~

~~Is to confront the burn skinning the eyes~~

~~To feel light scrape across the space inside~~

Wherever the eye chooses to rest

Inertia

The radiator bowed
from the tree's swift embrace
would steam   ~~hiss~~
& explode in seconds
but the snow   descending
not the snow   ~~(warming the slush)~~
that broke the car from the road
ripped it   ~~(straight)~~
through the curve
dampens as it descends
the back window trickling
having exploded   toward the front seat
your face a corsage
scarlet against the windshield
fissured & stained   but intact

Skin & Stain

He believes what he must
believes in blister & sun
frets over skin & its smooth
as a way to stave off the within

Sometimes the grass raises
a welt   a receiving ground
for what bites   digs   flares
where earth & air conspire to join

Everything outside combines & conspires
to ail he who believes & believes
the bitter & the sour taking over
more space than they need on the tongue

This spreading a small part
of what he believes is meant to erase
him from what he neither knows nor loves
but has been given against his will

If a machine could fix this
he would build or buy it
if an engine could ignite & solve
that engine would be his

The skin rebels daily & soaks
in what works to kill its host
a parasite writhing with parasites
the body totters & finds itself lost

The darkness there pools from the inside
invades everything like light
& the skin slips itself from the body
sunk at last & at last a ghost

Else ensure
a sordid
depart.

A framed
& fetid body
with wire
inside
its gut—

no skin

only scar

The Disfigured

here funereal & sleeved, the lack
of pressure at the wound's zipperish
opening will yield a rush of fluid
no bandage can squelch: cake the gash
with ash, rake it with anti-bacterial foam
& rinse. The bite will be intense
but quick, you'll forget the feeling within
the month. The shock of all that red,
though, will stay until the plaque in your brain
wipes it away, along with the names
of your progeny, your street, most parts
of your body, & so on, until even "name"
holds nothing but the space it occupies
on the page, in the air, until you look at yourself
in the mirror and see a figure there.

Broken tooth

forgotten in the precipice of snag,

bury yourself before forces
marshal new growth into wagons
married to twigs & stones,

try darkness on against the odds
of gain, & turn in your hole
for each promise made, & buried.

The adherence to rules as such
augurs well for you, fallen sparrow
burning on a wave. Unbuckle

yourself from your deeper truth,
consider the hypotenuse drawn
as T. sweeps into the room

bursting with light & remorse
for the living god shipped home
undone by bliss.

He would have blessed your pain
with an ardor more often reserved
for sicker creatures,

would have pulled the hurt
stirring at the root, sent
the throbbing packing. Forget

the wit that swells with wine
& cross yourself, unblessed one,
for the air says it's time to dress

for starker days. All else breaks
in the balance. All else hangs.

From the Bottom

"Burnished," when applied to limbs,
    refers you to furniture, or wood
    at least, a hint the skin has been burned
    beyond the human, & then beyond.

Necessary for the removal of skin
    from a burnished limb is an implement
    sharper rather than duller, wieldy
    & willing to dig without displacement.

The scrape of flint on a burnished limb
    —if you say "arm" you must mean it—
    resembles, no doubt, a chisel (of iron?)
    that furls what's before it, away.

The point of whatever has been lost
    between the stasis of the burnished limb
    & its movement away from the rest
    of what you have identified as skin,

the skin of a burnished limb,
    is to bring to bear the thought of bone
    & how it relates or, better, responds
    to its covering uncurling from it

flake by flake & amassing, forceless,
on the floor, the floor you will describe
as cement or concrete, at least
rug- and wood-less, the wood being

the skin of the burnished limb,
until the skin is just another piece
of your household furniture.

~~Disease unsavory in the first-person.~~
~~I am so impolite.~~
~~Discard me like the bump I am.~~
~~Chalk my body there on the street.~~
~~Maybe a pair will rut in my outline.~~
~~Maybe someone will sleep there.~~
My form at last useful at last.
~~Do not mention the rain.~~
~~Call the forensics artist a god.~~
~~Check his watch for the time of death.~~
Watch the rain cleanse for good.

The politics of posture & grip & syllable count
The retinue of flesh called to mind
The potential   acquaintance or otherwise
The presence of will in the act involved
The frequency of it   the motivation
The dangers of folklore   the dangers
The codes of behavior in the acts involved
The validity of choice of subject   of movement
The reason for darkness   for dampness
The cross forged & embedded in the wall
The furnishings   the view   the company not kept
The sounds outside   the sounds within
The length of time from start to fin-
ish   the length   the time   the finish

Rooms

There are rooms that know you, rooms you know
& can name, rooms that rise & stutter
into view if you stare long enough.
Rooms where nothing happened
but in your head, where the world went on
apart from you, you trying to rise to it.
Rooms with walls of white blocks,
one window, the only sound the bang
bang banging of the headboard
against the wall, your bed still.
The room where the bed fell on you,
the room where the hand going down
was not your own, the groping tongue
the proof. The room you talked your way
out of, four men of monosyllables,
thick arms & necks flushed pink,
closing in, emptying the air between.
The room where you were walked in on,
the room where you were the walker,
both times the last time in that room.
The room with no door, a woman
across the threshold, you crawling to her,
over her to the bathroom to press your cheek
against the white, your name
an indictment among stalls.

The room the sun never touched,
the sound of cars dropping you to sleep,
your pupils large & hungry for light.

Tied to the radiator
all winter

flagrant pesticide

Ankled discus-
flesh

silver nickel
another
flappish evil

Into the ditch
the blades
scrub & scrape

skeleton keyed

the personnel

Long distance
sight-
line:

the ghost
steals from
his casket

when the kiss

Dead Aesthetic

Already part gravel
the frog in the tire track
another weed to pull

lingerer on the outskirts

margin melting into the ditch

snuggled beneath a garden stone

between new & old

the issue of funding not

nature & what it suffers

sky that tilts with the trees

up to the gutter

& the driveway buckled

& running down the hill

signage all wrong

when the ground was cleared

the sun right back at the sun

of god the father developer

in his razing of all

where pavement meets pavement

& the black widow's nest

the finished road jolts

& then what

worth discussing here where

will dominate the monolog

to bring the eye down

droopy on the porch

by something buried

almost to the stop

markers of what's lost

& the roads were so new they shone

a middle finger in the face

father who failed

what unfolded before him

Stung air   airless
spider on the glass—

pet the no-
spider on the glass

Glaze the carpet's
streaks

            ferment

What is meant
by crowd control

in the pit
in which bodies swirl

Forsake the floor
for the stands

stand there with the cripple
& his crutches

Even the designated
driver

stares at the arrow
pulsing   not blinking

Even the designated driver
is pulsing   unblinking

The red light in front
now overhead in front

Saturated sheet—
he who hates

still delivers

For two dollars a tab
he delivers

Still he who hates
hates you

the I who writes

The foot
a hand

sabre-
toothed limb

What of the bodies'
motion   the view from above

Down there
all

was lost

Up here

the I
was lost

II.

& suddenly the music he wrote to
became a thing to remark on
not just to write to.   Not just a series of chords
                                                        & words
                        disappeared almost
                                            as soon as
                        they move through.

This brand of razor has not been tested on kittens
the only blood it draws is pure human cheek blood
the styptic pencil licks the gash inserts its non-
genetically modified acid into the wound.

The self-loathing the music lacks
I expand into a treatise
on animal testing.   Flay me right off
                                        & call me Marsyas /
                        yank that skin
                                    & wrap it
                        around my zeb roller.

mind a cluster of wet feathers stuck to a grate between curb and street

A thumb in his anus /
a finger in his ass
: the difference.   Confrontation
                                          und evasion.

The American girl   minor tennis star ████████
████   visits you in ████████   a long stay at the bar
bored   you know she is breaking up her trip from a
state further south to a state further north but clings
nevertheless and you missionary on the couch in the
spare room beside the dogs' crates   cannot remember
if the dogs were there or elsewhere   excited.

Anything received
as a gift
must be shared.   A sneeze caught

                                                    for good

                        by a sweatered arm.

The summer your ▮ father gave you an eighth of mushrooms
to watch his nephew for an afternoon   vestiges of an eight-
ball ▮▮▮▮▮▮▮▮▮▮▮▮▮▮▮▮▮▮▮ still on his nose   Belly's
Star on repeat until morning   the speed limit sign a white
corona right there on the side of the road   the narrow condo
streets the trees framing the night sky   and ▮▮▮▮▮▮▮
▮▮▮▮▮ you leave for ice cream and shear the sign off
its crepe paper post   find two hundred dollars flapping from
the money machine ▮▮▮   but that was another summer   in
another state.

Nothing solid exits the body
for the water
waiting stupidly below.   I have some bad news

                                                    it's about X.

                                    ~~He didn't make it.~~

The summer after the winter I fell from the ski lift dope
was the glue that held me to the people I was with   when
I chose the ▬▬▬ in front of me instead of the one far
away I realized my most common mode is failure   I loved
every one I left and still left because that   at least   was
motion   and I forgot more quickly than I recovered from
what I left behind.

II.

      drifting through the back yard
                         without a dress

along the third broken window
                    hair full of glass

      nothing in her arms
                          only a sheet on her back

despite the ladder still falling

III.

She turned from the soapy dishes
bent to unzip

▮▮▮▮▮▮▮▮▮▮▮▮▮▮▮▮

—I had been pushing.

There I am in the movie on the blanket on a lawn   her
tongue in for the movie the razorburn soothed for a
second by her spit she spits twice ~~for the movie~~   the first
dribbled in   the second deadcenter easing the tongue's
passage up.

One wouldn't go down ▮▮▮▮ and one
▮▮▮▮▮▮▮▮▮▮▮▮▮▮▮▮▮▮▮▮
wouldn't let me go ▮▮▮▮▮▮

—in both cases I felt ██████
destroyed.

One would let me touch the edge
but not go in, and one
would not let me anywhere near.

Neither wanted to fuck, but one did.

IV.

Though Christ was there much of the time
he is not welcome here.

                                        last night he could not make it

started driving on the motorway

                                        photographs in files

            sparked as he grazed it

                                    and he came right down

V.

The summer when the doctor at the clinic told me I had
herpes and I had been ██████ and knew somehow she
had been ██████ but there was the diagnosis   the hot
the itching red   I let her pray for me   wondered about
divine contagion   went online and saw a sexless future
went to another doctor   80 bucks to learn I had crotch
rot nothing sexual about it   let her ██████ me until the
pack ran out.

In the hotel room in ██████████ I nearly jumped
through the window having heard a noise in a dream
of attack and protection and went to bar the door but
bounced off the glass twelve stories up and made it to the
door anyway to hold it to   and ██ ████████████
████████████████   were there silent behind me
to pull me back to bed.

The going away party was for me and you were told you had ▓▓▓▓▓▓▓▓▓▓▓▓▓▓▓▓▓▓▓▓▓▓▓▓▓▓▓▓▓▓▓▓ for a short time and we felt indignant together the next morning though I was more hungover than indignant throwing up in the toilet until dinnertime and missed lunch with your family whom I would never see again and the next day I left you at the airport ▓▓▓▓▓▓▓ ▓▓▓▓▓▓▓▓▓▓ by choice and with difficulty   and now when I try to remember I cannot remember anything but the food.

VI.

Dust mites dig into me   flare my skin.

There's a difference between *dig* & *bite*.
These dig as they bite.
There's a difference between knowing
what you're talking about & caring.

Sing pollywollydoo all day.

VII.

All I remember of Nebraska is the vomit as it whipped
back toward the car   dappling the passenger side
finished all the coke in Boulder the night before   woke
up on some guy's couch   that photo on the porch   an
hour before

VIII.

                      To set a bone

that's been popped.

                             A shoulder untied

to a center.

An embolism & you're down.
A muscle tears in your back & you're down.
A ligament in your ankle, pop, & you're down.
A kick in the groin & you're down.
Aeschylus done in by a tortoise shell.
Montaigne's brother killed by a tennis ball.
You think you're strong but cannot lift
yourself by yourself.
Hence the importance of community.
Pack your bags, I'm moving in.

On the way to my apartment I never moved into   everyone
was evicted before I arrived   he was driving my car and the
headlights made a cat appear   he braked and pulled so hard
the car spun until it was facing the way we'd come   next time
kill the cat I said   but maybe it was a deer.

IX.

split in half
down to the root
itself snapped
from its anchor in

but not before
we're numb from ear
to chin
open

toothsmoke
jawwrench
bloodroot
gumclot

split in half
down to the root

X.

The pressure drops migraines me
I cough & one side of my head
a gunshot wound warm front & rain
left temple between vise ends
remove it please remove me from me

The summer before the coke nosebleeds the nosebleeds
were from something else   foreign matter in my head
three teeth pulled and no headache   the girl   nothing
happened   you took to a baseball game that night
nothing happened   a week later you drove her with
the top down into a thunderstorm on I-64   wet and
laughing   nothing happened.

XI.

With nothing to say   except through wine
we drank & smoked   until the edges smoothed
& she turned on a side   to invite me in
& my body obliged   though so unclear
about what it was   it was trying to do

XII.

Every dog deserves an elegy
        when it comes home from the oven
& is placed with sadness & pride
        on the mantle or some other shelf
to be dusted weekly for a while
        then monthly then not at all
& when the man who was the boy
        who loved the dog so much
he walked through snow to a phone
        to hear how she died & stood
in the snow at the corner's only phone
        to cry & remember & return
returns home a decade after
        & thinks to look for the tin
with the bag with the ashes inside
        he finds it on a shelf in a closet
where nothing else from his childhood
        is.

III.

Aubade

At the hour when sons consider the killing
of fathers,
        when dogs start to call
from their fences, half-acres & runs,
cardinals & finches teetering on the lips
of water bowls, metal that seizes too fast,
while cats press their stomachs to the soil
between house & hedge, & birds descend
like one too many shawls in a nest of wind—

the sun is "mostly" out at that hour,
the hour men live to forget when love occludes
the wound & the hunger that strung them
through each afternoon, sick lapse
in a life of lapses, failures to come to terms
with what moves nowhere, never comes,
but lust cannot be blamed for forgetfulness
(the twenty thousandth bottle of wine,
the hundred thousandth beer, shot of bourbon,
sweet culprits in the mind's many distractions).

This hour is not ushered in by the barking
that rebounds through the neighborhood,
is not illuminated by it, but is coeval with the sound,
simply a daily occurrence, on both counts—

the anger/hunger of sons, the "insane" frenzy of dogs—
though to take these words as reminder
of a hatred that has lost its harbor
would be to relinquish your hold
on the day that is already making good
on its threat to slip away from you.

As Difficult as Rain,

the snow on the glass as it melts.

Another border to ignore by crossing.

But why not stop
                    & turn to squint
at the streaks as they dry to burden,
wreck the window, make it less.

Why not focus on the failure of glass
to guide the eye through,
watch the snow harden

& not fall.

The pigeon trailing me
        from transformer to transformer has dropped
beneath my line of sight.

The orchard conceals
        assassin past, killer waxen orbs flourish
in this moribund aura.

A lowdown sun cannot muscle
        its way anywhere. I walk the river, frozen axis,
its tracks no altius of grace.

The sudden cold milks the darkness
        stellar, an apple shatters the surface
of the ice below:

a ripple from here to nowhere,
        mournful white road to nowhere.

The tower with its clock & flag
clicks & flaps above the riverlet
as you wait & ply your brain
with caffeine & wait with the hole
in your arm & its attendant bruise,
the rash aching, eating your skin
& swelling it so your arm limps along
with the rest of you, the flag with its clock
& tower shifts & points somewhere new,
pushing the shell (that's you) from your mind
& replacing it with the hornet assaulting
coffee dregs, the copter passing over,
the women passing, the postman, the river
whose name embraces its span, the river
whose water you can't see drink or drown in.

Night Is a Bird,

a crucible mid-flight
& flaming,
a trail of air
breaking air,
molecules blossom
as they burst
& fly.
I walk back to the hotel alone.

Nocturnal Angle

From my rented window
the upper Empire
State Building is naked
& emptied.
The missing teeth
of the lesser,
nearer buildings
lick me awake.
Tonight, sleep
is that distant spire.

Is there any thing not broken,
any part not about to break?
The question snaps. The line
cracks where it should be whole.
The chair in splinters, the sidewalk
in tatters. Bodies in pieces.
Because of the weight? gravity
& inertia yanking everything
apart? Everything belongs in pieces,
earth says, you try to hold everything
together, always have, & still
you fail, always will, your failure proof
that rot is too advanced for you, too far
ahead, or down, like strata, too patient,
like a fossil, which you collect & kill
in the collecting. Even your dust
shatters. Even your air.

no promise there, sequestered, belief
a crack in the world's festering:
the nightmare descends, intends
to scrub out your eyes & leave steel
wool behind, your teeth in pieces
on the pillow, spine scattered
across the sheets, graveyard of dust
mites & bits of skin, spit, hair.
The pus will not flush the dead matter.
The pus will not clean the sheets.
A mongrel will limp into your room
& remove the toes from your good foot
as you pray in your sleep to slide
over the edge. So easily over an edge.

A smattering of cirrus, no rain
       that day.
The cars slipped through the town's
       one stoplight,
circled the gravel track around
       the gravesite.
Who was given a handle of the casket
       to guide it
to the tent, the body's
       new roof?
Whose eyes were open during the prayer?
       Who refused?
Who wept &, weeping, raised a finger
       as if to curse?
The dirt spilt into the fresh hole,
       filled mouths.
They choked on what they could not swallow.
       The flesh

Inertia

Pallborne on a metal frame

                    —rack of jolted eddies—
you watch hard the tree

                / telephone pole divide

wonder almost casually
how steep the bank

                how far the drop

but the tree stops you fast

                    sends you
sideways

until the car is part of the ground

                        & you unbuckle
to the music of glass thrashing down

The remnants   the matter   the mulch that sticks
adheres because it stacks what it cannot fix
a fever of water intact for minor seconds
a veer   a failure   this slumber that begins
& begins   works to wake what is waking
a line   the level   align every plane with a plane
the house aslant   a slant of wood & weather
light when it finds a way through door or pane
the floor   the wall   the angles jeer   shudder
the house slants   slides   slips   sinks   shaking
the skin within strains   rips   an open thing
that begins as remains & ends as no thing

Unload

A fault line in the linear.
A threat to "to advance."
A nick in every surface.
A page missing from the book.
A ladybug's dying scent.
A light that blinks when on.
A slab that shucks off paint.
A plank that does not meet.
A nailhole in the ceiling.
An outlet that will not spark.
An unravel in the carpet.
A welcome infestation.

Elegy, Post-Paternal

Dead a weekend
& a day
before his best friend
found him
on the floor
of his apartment's
one bedroom
where he'd been sleeping
that year
to calm the hurt
in his back,
he'd swollen
beyond human
when I saw him
three hours before
he was to be flown
in his coffin
two states down
& burned,
scattered
across the land
he'd hated
until he'd grown
& still hated
but now had no choice

but to embrace
&, dead, own.

Elegy, Presentable

We gathered by the aviary. One cried
before the cake was cut & carried
to everyone present. I cut the cake,
carried a piece to everyone present.

The woman who cannot see   hear   eat
was wheeled to where you sat.
Did not notice   the crowd or the occasion.
A few knelt to whisper   pet   caress
she who had sunk below the floor
of her mind, to dwell there
& never return. I knelt.

How to celebrate a life in the presence
of the dead? How to keep that death
from rubbing off onto the less-than-dead?
We ignored what we were   will become,
crammed cake into ourselves
& smiled.   Happy death.

Elegy, Flailing

One must not be dying to gasp,

one must not gasp to die.

I have a destination in mind

but am not sure how to get there

& Jeff Buckley's broken "Hallelujah,"

which begins with a gasp

& ends with a long strum,

which I thought might point the way

or suggest a direction,

has ended & left me weighing

the lines I wrote earlier,

on another piece of paper

    —no longer look up when we hear a plane,

    follow a fire engine, anything with a siren,

    to see the cause of the commotion,

    press to a window to watch a train,

    stay there until the last car can no longer be seen—

& now I think of death by drowning,

a river death, The River's Edge,

what that means for the skin,

how it must cancel the care

taken to protect from the sun,

aging & what it does to the ways
we move through the world
my subject here

> —not death, not the body failing
> —not elegy, flailing

but a look at what happens after childhood
is a constellation of discrete moments
recalled amid a general blur,
nostalgia tremens,
after the first fuck has dropped
from the mind's rearview,
when we no longer look skyward
at the sound of a plane,
follow a firetruck
to the cause of the commotion,
press to a window to watch a train,
stay there until the last car has moved
beyond the point our eyes can reach,
after interior math has become rote,
recognizing & arranging letters
without pause—tiny actions
that we once thought impossible
now invisible, without friction.

But friction is what slows us
as we move toward the dying,
friction is what slows us
as we move toward the dying.
Without it we will slide effortless
into our own end. Without it
we will slide without effort
without pause with or without
a gasp at the end, our end.

Not a whisper when we arrived, but a roar
there to greet us—two continents rubbing.
To yawn at the sight would have meant scrubbing
oneself from an outcrop along the shore,
we thought, so sure of the power that comes with size
here where enormities are said to collide.

We were being held, & the choice—suicide
or murder—was not ours to make: how one dies
& to what music, in what & whose interests,
can be composed beforehand but not willed.

What, with time, could we have thwarted
at the coast of what, where nothing rests.
The edge framed those who would be killed.
The coast aborted us, we aborted

the coast.

Anaesthesia

As if drowning occurs only at the shore, I drop
to a knee, ease my self onto one side, to thrash.

My self has done this to me & no one can care,
for to care would be to allow, & there is no one

to allow here. The ones here do not care to allow.

A bridge: it gathers me & the water, makes
my self a bank for the river. The bridge knows

how to gather, to make a bank of nothing,
which I am.
          Come to me, watch it work.

The day, that open sore, refusing to heal into night,
we hole up in the corner of the cellar, a pit of clay
tilting up at each side.
                  The water heater awake despite
the absence of bodies in the house (there is no need),
it builds, then boils, & the air around slides toward itself
(as if the air has self) & dips below the floor above (nails
dangling) to sweep us from where we're crouched, afraid
the house will lift & spin across the sky like metal
wagon wheels breaking in the sidewalk.
                        Water cooks, would pool.
You weep into my hands at the wind's first rush.
                            We feel
the pull from without, the slip in pressure that precedes the fall.
See the drop descend to hang then rise, to rescind, return.
The water will rust, the clay, the red, will swallow us
as the windows withdraw & the rafters (but not the nails) burn.

Easter / Evening

How delicate the world is   (how soon)
Thusly she knelt beside me

A voice stepping over the quickest spiders
Two worms having worked their way inside

A figurine gesturing on the worn carpet
A breeze beneath the baseboards

The windows (there are four) sweat
What the rain has left the air

A family of cardinals invites itself
The carved jug full of seed

How many glasses on the floor
Frenzied propositions shamed into pieces

Lightning horizontal the night before
Crossing the sky before striking

My delicate world in pieces   (this morning)
Nothing falls apart

IV.

Wreckage

As I branched out

     & into,

   swollen under

the weight

    of consideration—

I was considering

      myself,

        was subject

& ob-,

           (was neither?)

a woman in view

     & viewer,

       & viewing her

self as viewer—

              I swelled to burst

-ing & was nothing with nothing

         happening to me.

II.

Have reduced lonesomeness to

Fragment of heartsickness for

Bartered a common scent before

Her chapter in static air

The sun instilled a desire like

Scratching the paint off the door

Forget the porcelain's crack in

Ass-swept field parade inside

Search party fruitful describe

Such dust the likes of which

III.

Separate ( ) the words.

Separate the words, please.

The end of *the end of*s
brings I where?

here on the cusp of *as*
& *like*, between

all this fucking
is.

IV.

Digest what causes
pain, in   ~~digest~~
pieces   ~~in pieces~~
what flutters your chest
& forces you onto
your other side, the muscles
around the heart hurt   ~~are swollen~~
the weak knee swollen
to the shin   ~~flusters~~
break it in
flag the pain as it moves   ~~broken~~
through you
arrest it before it
do you in

V.

To what I will say ( )
what will I say ( )
past the how of its ( )
I will say what ( )
has been said ( )
but not said ( ) by me:
what I say will be un-
said ( ) un-
derstood as unsaid ( )
by me ( ) nothing like silence
( ) this nothing like silence.

VI.

what if there is no continuing the disturbance
I feel in the air around me would collapse like
so many cardinals dropped from the sky
by weak persistence & abandoned in the fog
of midday the turd in the dog's mouth
it won't let go of its grip on what is
loosening the calling home to check in
to what abnormalities persist on time
& again the ants resurface ten
feet further into the yard's distracted
ground a series of stumps requiring an-
nihilation by scattered pellets the ants
will carry back to their babies the queen
two cats at either corner of the property
back a third into the third before each
takes a rock between the eyes

VII.

two shelves moving create a third shelf an in
       between
ice in ripped halves gropes toward water in
       stead
an animal covered in animal fur bleats in
       human
sounds the land worried lets go of what's un
       said

the placenta dragged into the moraine's in
       constant
stretch the animal forgets what it is & in
       vites
the sky's falling through water's weak in
       stant
glorious so glorious this birthscene this un
       scene

VIII.

Obscene fortune trust fund baby bunker whom to feed
when you're the king of feed banter frolic as if grass
had no feelings hourglass physiques belie stuporous
mothballed pockets glitter on your lashes crawlspace
fuckspace everywhere a shitspace everyone a shit
lashed to the foremast no sailor would pardon undone
sphincter muscles unloose your seed upon the sea
doctrines wet wit dis moneyshot riddled like cheese
dreams halfchewed & spit onto linoleum to lick clean
come morning the lightbulb dangling sees though broken
every flaw in the structure every zit on your chin
the mole you carry so richly to the security counter
wait for the door behind to close before you reach
for the door in front the camera needs a minute to size

IX.

Execute the stump & the termites emerge
as the thread,
grass tufts violent as bricks against bone.

Call forth the energy to cut the gatherings
down, call forth
call forth, your voice so your own.

X.

A semblance of seriousness settles into the patches you've laid in the concrete

Domestic bravura showcasing your freckled muscles encroaching on tan lines

Foreign accents are welcome especially when the subject is coffee   or futons   or wine

Donations accepted in the parking-lotted dumpster 24/7   no receipt

The tree with the vine-covered base must be felled before winter & its winds

A retaining wall to keep the clay from caving in

Woodchips & mulch & weeds & gravel   vines & ties & fenceposts & wires

The squirrel's nest attracts a dog a bird   the pot-bellied pig its nose in the dirt

A lesson in erosion brought to you by the land   the treefort's termites pinched by ants

The widow in the house behind you has placed a pipe to drain what she sprays

The angle saturates your hands

XI.

The vines, let them rain their sap on me,

                               raise welts, blister.

Wrists, forearms, triceps, chest, stomach, thighs

                                     all itch to a burn.

To peel the skin away, scrape it into bits,

                               scald a normal skin.

The scars, too, will itch.

XII.

A door kicked into its jamb

Fire ants cross the walk

Pleasure exists only in mulch

The roots will not dissolve

Careful of run-off & sick

The road though paved is rough

I track my tongue along a nail

Gasoline settles the garage

I pump pesticides into my half-acre

This is the gardenia's week to shine

BRIAN HENRY is the author of six previous books of poetry, including *Quarantine* (Ahsahta). His translation of the Slovenian poet Tomaž Šalamun's *Woods and Chalices* appeared from Harcourt in 2008, and his translation of Aleš Šteger's *The Book of Things* appeared from BOA Editions in 2010.

Ahsahta Press

Ahsahta Press

NEW SERIES

MODERN AND CONTEMPORARY POETS OF THE AMERICAN WEST SERIES

Many of the books in this series are available for download at
http://scholarworks.boisestate.edu/ahsahta/

This book is set in Apollo MT type with Bauer Bodoni titles
by Ahsahta Press at Boise State University
by Thomson-Shore, Inc.
Cover design by Quemadura.
Book design by Janet Holmes.

AHSAHTA PRESS

2011

JANET HOLMES, DIRECTOR

JODI CHILSON, MANAGING EDITOR

KAT COE   GENNA KOHLHARDT

CHRIS CRAWFORD   BREONNA KRAFFT

TIMOTHY DAVIS   MATT TRUSLOW

CHARLES GABEL   ZACH VESPER

KATE HOLLAND   EVAN WESTERFIELD